PRAI[...]

The American Midwest, a [...]
for too many of us a place [...]
buckle of the Rust Belt, or a bundle of interchangeable Flyover States. Sue
Burton's masterly long poem reminds us that those who toiled in the Rust
Belt factories played a pivotal role in the creation of what used to be called
the American Dream, and were among the earliest victims of its betrayal.
In a poem that is part documentary in the mode of Muriel Rukeyser's *The
Book of The Dead* and part a biographical study of the author's parents
that recalls Rita Dove's *Thomas and Beulah*, Burton searchingly—and
searingly—explores the impact of a bloody 1937 steel strike on her
hometown of Massillon, Ohio: the lives that it changed, the lives that
it ruined, and the ongoing legacy of that event, one that continues to
haunt the poet. *Little Steel* is a work of fierce tenderness and consummate
ambition, one in which the personal and the historical commingle and
fuse. And, as Burton repeatedly reminds us, we cannot read *Little Steel* as
a form of elegy: it is instead a work of hard-won—and deeply resonant—
praise.

—David Wojahn, author of *For the Scribe*

Sue Burton's *Little Steel* gives vivid color and beautiful form to the lives of
those who extracted metal from the rocks of the earth and to the bygone
world they created. Sometimes so gentle, sometimes so angry, but always

intimate and intricately well-informed, this honest and moving study in verse is at once a great gift to the reader and a noble tribute to its subjects. It should be read and read closely by all who wish to understand how labor and labor struggles have shaped our world.

> —Ahmed White, author of *The Last Great Strike: Little Steel, the CIO, and the Struggle for Labor Rights in New Deal America*

Little Steel is amazingly successful in its project of interweaving social and political history with private family drama. Through many acts of investigation and many painful memories, Burton leads us to feel depths of political and moral and psychological significance in the story of a labor strike in Massillon, Ohio, in 1937. She shows us how the arenas of the public and the personal intersect, and mirror each other. She is a bold and resourceful poet, bravely seeking meanings in charged images from the past, and her obsessive quest becomes very moving—as a search for renewal of love between daughter and father, as a struggle for "women's health" in the largest sense, and as an affirmation of belief in community. *Little Steel* is a long poem of rare ambition and cumulative power.

> —Mark Halliday, author of *Thresherphobe*

LITTLE STEEL

LITTLE STEEL

FOMITE...

POEMS
SUE D. BURTON

Copyright © 2018 Sue D. Burton
Cover and book design: W. David Powell

Cover art: Philip Evergood, *American Tragedy*, 1937, oil, 29.5 x 39.5, private collection, photograph courtesy Terry Dintenfass, Inc.

Interior art: Paul Raphael Meltsner, *Death of a Striker*, 1935, lithograph, 10.75 x 14.5 and *Industrial Landscape*, 1935, lithograph, 10.25 x 14.5, from the collection of Thomas Sodders, of the Labor Education & Arts Project Inc., Cleveland, Ohio.

All rights reserved. No part of this book may be reproduced in any form or by any means without the prior written consent of the publisher, except in the case of brief quotations used in reviews and certain other noncommercial uses permitted by copyright law.

ISBN-13: 978-1-944388-51-5
Library of Congress Control Number: 2018xxxxx

Fomite
58 Peru Street
Burlington, VT 05401
www.fomitepress.com

CONTENTS

ONE
3

LITTLE STEEL

Little Steel / Marry in Red / Steel Town /
Republic's Girl / The Reunion /
Hold That Tiger / Tigers / Gray Cat /
Marry in Black / Red /The Headless Woman /
Clean Fill / Praise / Highway to Nada

TWO
55

BACK HOME FROM NYC & OHIO, SITTING ON MY FRONT STEPS, I'M LOOKING OUT AT THE VERGE, THAT GRASSY STRIP BETWEEN THE SIDEWALK & THE STREET—IN OHIO WE CALLED IT THE DEVIL'S HIGHWAY—& I'M THINKING ABOUT AMERICA & ART & THE DEAD STEEL TOWN WHERE I GREW UP & THE "MILL"—NOW A STORAGE YARD FOR FRACKING PIPE, HUNDREDS OF MILES OF STEEL PIPE

Paul Raphael Meltsner, *Death of a Striker*, 1935

ONE

LITTLE STEEL

Let us praise Fulgencia Calzada, shot
in the back of the head. Let us interrogate the bullet.
Oh, but the strikers threw a rock.

And let us praise Nick Vathias — or Vadios
or Vadlas — gunned down at the door to the strikers' kitchen:
Excusable homicide.

Praise the Union who took up a collection —
Calzada's BB-blasted four-foot cross
is over near the fence,

though what's become of Vathias's cross,
so we could check the spelling?
Praise the Erie Street Cemetery

that dips and rises for acres, gray slabs smack-dab
in front of black marble monuments the size
of mobile homes — a far cry

from Rose Hill where my father is buried, dead-level
cow field on the other side of town
where the Great Equalizer has stomped

the graves, heelprinting
identical flat metal plaques
and pop-up metal vases.

But behind Erie's mausoleum, the footstones
of Section 4 are flanked by lumps and sags.
Even in death, the worst view

in town — the west border plunging
to rambling, defunct
Republic Steel.

So praise Betty — Betty, the furnace
(and Betty, my best friend in high school) —
ten million dollars, fired up

in October 1926,
"hundreds of steel men in attendance"

gaping like medieval bumpkins

at Reims Cathedral. Big Betty —
one swell Lady! —
processed 6.5 million tons of iron

before she was banked for the last time
in 1965.
Razed in 1974.

Praise the girders, the pilings,
the stainless pots and pans, the roller bearings,
the hand rails, the chassis, the gears,

the road signs, the crankshafts, the tankers,
the hulls, the kitchen sinks, the bread knives,
the bed springs, the train tracks,

the lorries, the DC3s —
Praise steel.
Praise Massillon steel.

MARRY IN RED

25 years from high school.
Last night's "Hold That Tiger" still reverberates —
we stood and ridiculously sang

before the buffet, and then again at midnight.
I can't decipher the Erie Street Cemetery map,
so follow a hillbilly Virgil —

a kid with an orange mustache, with a twang
I got knocked out of me when I was ten.
We keep 'er up by selling graves, he says.

What if you run out of plots? I say.

He waves toward a new section across the street —
fresh dead maintaining the old,
the infallible formula of Social Security.

Section 4, he says, is the only place
where the fill has sunk. *The foreign side*, he says,

kicking at one of the mounds.

They came from Italy, from Greece, from
Slovakia, from Spain. They came up from West
Virginia (my mom said, *Don't let on that's*

where your Dad's from). They came
from the South, though blacks had to settle
in "The Bottoms."

The mill. The mill. Blood
brothers, they married the mill.
Marry in red, wish yourself —

Battalions of smokestacks keeping them
true, big shotguns on end.
Marry in blue —

Veil of ash, of unremitting
heat, acres of soot: gritty wedding-cake
basilica. A promise

big as a city, brick, looming, separated
by a moat — the Tuscarawas River —
from the "good side of town."

Some days the sun cut red through the haze.
And some days she didn't bother.

O, but it *was* a dream — in 1937, they fisticuffed
for $5/day, a 40-hour week. By 1986, $600/
week, time-and-a-half overtime. If —

§

Interview with Uncle Bob:

Of course, you had your foreigners that did the rough jobs down there, like chipping and scarfing, which is real bad for your health. They lived on the other side of town, over in Columbia Heights. They'd come in by the hundreds, and there'd be 20, 25 of 'em living in one house this size. They'd have bunks in the basement and little cupboards for their bread, and they'd save every dime and send it back to Italy. Then when they'd made enough money, they'd go home — without any teeth! They'd all lose their teeth from the acid fumes in the soaking pits. If they didn't quit young, they were dead — 'cause it killed 'em, sure as you're a foot tall.

§

I got to know all the whores up there. I was a salesman for the local light company. Every year we put out a package real cheap that promoted electricity. So I'd go up to The Heights and I'd sell these girls 5, 6 packages apiece. They'd send them back to West Virginia, Carolina, wherever their families were 'cause they had money they didn't know what to do with. I won the contest every year. Nice kids. During the day when I was doing business with them, they were just like talking to you. Take it from your Uncle Bob, they weren't any different at all.

§

In '37, Republic went out on strike, so the cops went up into Columbia Heights and shot off a bunch of bullets. A shame — we got bad national publicity out of the thing. And it sort of stuck with us that this was a radical union town. The mill wanted the strike broke and they — well, they hired everything. Even an armored car from the Canton Police. Major Curley, he was in charge of the whole doggone thing. His son was strong in the union. It was bad, him on one side of the fence and his son on the other.

§

When they came across the viaduct, it was more than just the city police. Some said there was coal and iron police. But they had the plant protection guarding the guys that were working. See, they brought over a whole bunch of Arabs and they were living in box cars down in the plant.

There were Arabs here?

They called them A-rabs. They were from Arabia or India or wherever they came from, but they ...

Republic brought Arabs in to work?

Yeah, Republic Steel brought in strike breakers and they brought 'em in railroad cars. So nobody knew they were in there. 'Course, the A-rabs didn't know anything about steel mills, so they didn't get a damn thing done. They were finally accepted. I mean, it was a known fact they didn't know what the hell they were brought in for. They didn't know anything about a strike. So afterwards, they migrated from the box cars and settled up in Columbia Heights.

STEEL TOWN

Worse than I remembered – every block
with boarded-up stores, leveled
gray lots. Some arsonist hasn't been

caught for a year, even gutted
the City Building where Rita's Beauty Parlor
was on the fifth floor for 23 years.

Rita had to cancel Mom out the day of the fire.
I look a sight, Mom phoned to tell me.
I can't bring myself to make the turn:

grounded like ocean liners impervious, at last,
to fire and flood and gypsy moths;
portholes protected with wire,

shattered anyway with well-aimed rocks;
barricaded gangways scrawled with red — *JOBS!*
up yours! suckee!

I have my father's CIO dues pin from the year
he worked at Republic. August 1941.
Did he get one every month?

Why did he keep it?
Why did he keep a loaded Derringer
under the work bench in the basement?

A bigger version of me — long skinny feet,
the hated freckles (they called him Turkey Egg
back on the farm). We let Mom do all

the talking (he, she says now,
had no father and never learned).
The unsaid was ours, a secret

handshake, a kind of poetry.
I was a tongue-tied child.
What did I know?

What do I know now,
pounding out words to convince him?

And of what?

That fifty-plus years ago he should have
taken on the law-and-order boys?

§

Oh, Sudie, you always sided with your Daddy.
Don't you like him anymore? Now that he's dead.
Why do I have to talk into that contraption?
Don't squinch my eyes? I look like a corpse?
Well... you brought that thing.
Here's my advice to my daughter: Don't

stir up trouble. Over talking to Uncle Bob —
don't believe a word he says. Dredging up
that awful strike. Of course we never talked of it
when you were a child. Ancient history
even then. Divided the town.
Best forgot.

Where was Daddy during the strike?

*He worked at the Chevy garage. Yes, his boss
was on the Law and Order Committee. Yes,
Grampa sold real estate. With an office downtown.
Grampa and Daddy would never shoot people.
Daddy was a hard worker.*

*What do you mean, where do you draw the line?
You worry me, Sudie. You and your
notions. We should never have sent you
to that fancy college.
Took out a second mortgage.
I remember one time Daddy and I came to visit —*

*I was wearing a cotton dress. All the other mothers
had on knit suits. We drove into Columbus
and bought me a suit. Your roommate Julie's mother
had a gold necklace with a little clock.
But you were just as pretty as Julie. You always
had such pretty hair. And now you say*

*money doesn't matter! My mother told me
it's just as easy to marry a rich man as a poor —*

I wish I'd listened to my mother.
When we built this house — you were five years old—
well, a shell of a house and no money
for a driveway or cupboards.

Oh, I'd say I've had a good life. But people
always try to take what's mine. Even now, old
and alone, and neighbors trying
to take what's mine. Even when I was a little girl.
That's why I sit in the dark — so no one
can sneak up behind.

REPUBLIC'S GIRL

Let us praise the interminable graveyards
Dad dragged me through as a kid, the long drives
down to Wheeling to the Palestine Christian Church,

the rutted red clay road up the hill
to Uncle Pete's farm where Dad grew up, Dad
with his notebook

penciling in names and directions.
Let us praise his example
of tracking the dead.

If what Swift said is true (all of us only fleas
on the backs of bigger fleas, biting away, *ad infinitum*),
if it's all just a matter of scale,

why can't my bigger flea be Santorini? — the lost Atlantis,
guidebook Eden, sky-blue sky. Why is my flea Massillon, Ohio,
dead steel town, U.S.A., truly deserving, but passed over

as the site for the Football Hall of Fame? —
where even the Cameo Grill's plate-sized Tigerburger
gave way to McDonald's.

Everybody's dad worked at Republic.
Everybody's dad was always out on strike.
Or talking strike.

My dad worked up at Goodyear, open shop.

When I was a kid, the town was known
for three things: the high school football team (State Champs
my senior year), the National Shrine of St. Dymphna,

and the numbers games on Erie and Main.
Massillon was thirty thousand then;
Tiger Stadium sat twenty-two.

§

St. Dymphna: one of those female saints
with a missing body part — her

head.

Cut off by her father when she
refused to marry him.
He didn't want anyone else to have her.

Well, everything's fair in love.
But who'd ever brag she's Massillon's
own — Republic's "girl"?

And who'd ever brag that the Headless Woman
at the Stark County Fair has been *Kept Alive
thru the Miracle of Science! See her Living Body*

without a Head!
But there she is: out on Erie Street, just past
the graveyard, at the Massillon State Hospital:

a padded red dress
propped in front of a plywood box with holes
for some carnie's arms and legs

to poke through. Fuzzy red anklets.
Red battery charger for a head, gold letters:
Wizard, 6 amp.

Let's interview the Headless Woman,
the *real* woman inside the box —
the one stuck back there in the dark,

who can't even go to the can
unless her boyfriend lifts her out.

§

Sometimes I think about what it's like inside St. Dymphna's head. Like I'm this tiny person inside her skull, and it's dark and nobody can see me or hear me, but I can see out and see everything that's happening.

Sometimes I'm in there watching St. Dymphna's father pick up his sword. And I say, Daddy, don't. But he keeps coming, and it's dark and nobody can see me or hear me, but I can see out.

I'm in there watching, and I keep saying, Daddy, don't. But he keeps coming, and he raises up his sword, and he's bringing it down. And I say, Daddy, don't! But he keeps coming and coming.

THE REUNION

Praise my old friend Betty, pretty as ever, henna
hiding the gray, who gets me out on the dance floor
doing the *shug*, who whispers that Ruth, our yearbook queen,

joined Right-to-Life and married a millionaire.
Who says, *I remember kneeling in the kitchen — Dad, Mom,
me and my sisters — saying the rosary so the union wouldn't strike.*

Who says, *No money coming in. Kids, rent. My dad
meaner than hell.* Who says, *It's not that I forgave.
But I began to understand.*

Who says, *What's the big deal, your dad
against the union? It's not* your *story — strikers
getting shot, that helpless saint.*

Who drives with me to Rose Hill, holds my elbow
as we walk the rows of identical markers.
Who says, *He's got to be here someplace.*

§

And with the severing of my head,
I lost all memory.

I forgot it was my mother
who governed the blade.

I forgot I had a father
who could've saved me, but couldn't.

No, I dreamed there was a father
who wanted to save me,

buried inside the father
ruled by the blade.

I forgot who was who,
who looked the other way.

I cannot find my father's grave.

§

When I'd left for the reunion, Mom warned me
not to talk to Ruth. Mom still thinks
I should've been yearbook queen — *and not*

just because I'm your mother. An abortion clinic
up in Akron, she'd heard on the radio, was bombed
last week. *Don't talk to Ruth*, she said.

Praise Ruth, whose mom — a twin to mine — was
a real purse-clutcher, twitchy, always checking out a room —
and loud, always saying weird things,

Ruth, who's glowing now, silk burgundy
befitting the wife of a millionaire, who says
Christ saved her marriage,

who when I say I work in "women's
health," reverts to her high school self,
reaches to pat my shoulder, stops

mid-air before the touch. Who says,
I guess we're on different sides of the fence.
Who says, *I hope you still like me.*

HOLD THAT TIGER

1947. *The Evening Independent*

Fair weather prevailing, Massillon is expected to have the largest rally in its history at Tiger stadium at 7:30 this evening when Philip Murray, president of the Council of Industrial Organizations and head of the United Steelworkers of America delivers his first speech in this city: *You could not have had a meeting in this beautiful stadium ten years ago tonight. Certainly your mayor wouldn't have been here then, nor the sheriff of your county. I doubt if you would have secured the services of your high school band, and I wouldn't have been here for the same reason that you wouldn't have been here.*

§

1986. *The Evening Independent*

2000 march through Massillon to get the plant back in operation.... *I never thought this would happen*, said Don Ely, who worked there 20 years, his father 30 years.... Retirees of

LTV Corp. and the Republic Steel Corp. were jolted Monday as news spread that their hospitalization, life insurance and Workers Compensation coverage was cut off by LTV.... USX, the old U.S. Steel, is stocking riot gear and tear gas in case of trouble....

Not many in Massillon feel pangs of regret for the recently departed. Newstat reportedly got $1.7 out of Enduro and McMarlin (LTV) testified he got $160,000 a year and a $50,000 bonus in January. Greenberg, the attorney, got, well, you know how much attorneys can get. Let's just say these three gentlemen won't be showing up in a soup line anytime in the next few years.

§

Down the west hill from Section 4, Republic's
dingy metal roofs
snake four or five city blocks

parallel to the cemetery. What does he
think, looking down there every day, the ghost
inside this grave who took a stand?

Grown sardonic over the years,
hoping for a belly laugh to free him
from this Ohio fog

into real death, does he
sit up on his cross and let the wind whiz
through the hole in his head —

or has Calzada poked his
holy head out of his sunken bed just
once since he dropped off, waking in 1947

sure he must be sleep-drunk, flabbergasted
at the sound of his own name blasting
across town from Tiger Stadium?

But then, hearing Murray's crackling speech
and the hurrahs, did he begin to
fancy himself a folk hero, pipedreaming

of the Tiger band marching with the Word

through thousands of Massillons all over America,
leading big Easter-type parades

like the ones he knew as a boy in Spain,
the high-stepping majorettes strutting
to the tune of "Hold That Tiger"?

§

Who am I, in this funk, to take on
the status quo? I could barely explain myself
at the reunion, as if I'd forgotten

my mother tongue. Ruth had her own souls
to save. Betty passed around pictures of her kids.
The two laid-off men at my table

changed the subject.

TIGERS

This poem will not hold any tigers.
It will not raise up the union martyrs.
It won't even solve the mystery of Nick Vathias's

four-foot missing tombstone. It will not bring
Philip Murray back to Tiger Stadium
or the beaming mayor or the stirring benediction

from Rev. Scully, chaplain of the National Shrine
of St. Dymphna, Patroness of Sleepwalkers
and the Possessed.

This poem will not return the union to its heyday.
It will not de-greed the greedy CEOs.
It will not bring back the mills.

It will not bring back my father or my father's
father. My father will never hear me say,
Don't tell me Calzada was a nobody.

*I don't care if he was just standing there
in the crowd, that he had "no options
anyway" — that he couldn't pass*

*like you with your good
English name.
I don't care how measly his last breath was,*

poor slob ambushed from behind. He was
there. *He* made *the crowd.*

And where were you, Hands-in-your-pockets,
when Patrolman "Submachine" Fellabom
gunned down some frightened unarmed man

for — what? — throwing a stone?
Where were you, Good Citizen Now-now-dear,
Trusty Foreman Yes-boss-yes-boss-yes?

GRAY CAT

I used to dream of a gray cat
disappearing into the snow, fat wet
flakes filling in its tracks. I wonder if

my father ever wanted to follow his
father, vanish into the hills of
West Virginia, *almost heaven.*

The dreams began in college, came in waves,
at first following close on Mom's reports
of my father's dizzy spells,

then preceding them like an aura —
sometimes false alarms.
I can't remember when the dreams

stopped — sometime after I got married,
before I got divorced, before he
did die.

I suppose there's something
to the timing. I began to steel myself.
And then, after his death, the onset:

my archives, my "informants" —
my fruitless returning.

MARRY IN BLACK

*I married your Daddy in a black satin dress. Sudie,
don't stand by the window, I'll tell you the story.
We ran off to Wheeling, didn't tell a soul.
The day after Christmas, 1931.*
Marry in black, wish yourself back.
It was the Depression. It was my best dress.

*We got married in a preacher's kitchen,
the preacher's wife in her housecoat, a year
to the day that Frank Faolain died.*
Marry in blue, love ever true.
*Don't lean on the bed, Sudie, don't give me that look.
Your Daddy was a good man, with sandy red hair.*

*But he was old, and a cold husband. Oh, now
I am old, too — how old am I now?
Frank Faolain had indigo eyes, hair black as time.
A brand new Packard, but it ran off the road.
What a life I could have had — my Frankie, he'd have
sailed me to Paris! Orchids and cinnamon tea.*

*On my soul, I wanted to die. And then poor Frankie
so broody in the grave — oh, what a drafty house
the preacher had, the windowpanes all rattling.
The porch door banged and banged.
Sudie, why do these things come back to me?
The wind always calls me by name.*

*You were so cross when you were a child, when I'd take
to my bed. You wanted your Mama to comb her hair.
Or did your Daddy put you up to it?
Frank Faolain was the only one who understood. Oh,
as though he were inside me. Nights
his face in the window —*

*We ran off to Wheeling, your Daddy and I.
My mother read our letters, but didn't tell the neighbors.
But the principal found out —
It was the Depression. Jobs were for men or for girls
with no husband. But your Daddy had no job.
Your Daddy was out of work.*

*They wouldn't let me empty out my desk.
My students made a petition with drawings of tears.
I want my pictures back: me standing with my class. But now
Frankie is here. And a white dress. And a beaded shawl,
with rosettes and ivy. Now I'll have a wedding in the church
and Mother will forgive me.*

*Don't stand by the window, you're blocking my light.
Crosspatch, crooked stick. Your face will freeze that way.* Marry
in red, wish yourself dead. *Revlon Revenesence cream is best.
Frankie is here. And the white dress, ruffles to the floor,
buttons at the wrist. I'll slip my arms into the sleeves.
He'll button me up, so many silk buttons up the back.*

RED

I'm five. My brother is thirteen.
My mother is throwing plates at my brother.
She's screaming, *You think I'm a whore!*
Red shards on the kitchen floor.

I'm six. Maybe I'm seven.
My mother is chasing my brother
with a butcher knife. I run upstairs. My father
sits in the living room, reading the paper.

I'm sixteen. My mother screams at my father.
She screams at me when I take his side.
She calls my friends if I'm not home by eight.
I don't have dates.

She gets my father to look at houses in other towns
because girls in Massillon get pregnant.
I'm seventeen. My mother won't go out alone.
She says Nazis are tapping our phone.

She won't let me talk to my boyfriend
because he has a German name.
I ask my father to take her to Dr. Meck,
but my father says, *Dr. Quack*.

§

Did my father shrink like this at night, into himself,
clenched fist beneath the sternum?
Did he lie awake, dreading the persistence

of the clock? Hours after he'd left for work,
I'd find his bedclothes still drenched.

THE HEADLESS WOMAN

Sometimes when I do my Headless Woman gig,
I think about the American dream.

In Britain, I hear they dream about the Queen.
And her little dogs. But over here —

you're roaming the halls of Washington High,
late, and you can't find the room

for your history final, having ditched
class for months, the books

long-gone, and you can't think of your history teacher's
name — Miss Somebody who got in bad

with the school board for thanking God in class
when Kennedy was elected.

What, me, Clio of Ohio, late for history?
The recurrent American dream.

Praise the sleepwalkers, always reaching
for something, punching in, punching

out, sometimes here in the dark I read their stories
with a flashlight. They sleep but they don't

dream. A "functional" problem. They walk,
they talk. They don't have dreams.

Did my father have dreams?
The litany of jobs — Goodyear Aircraft: tool maker,
plastics, foreman. Before that, WPA (roads),

mechanic, machinist, railroad fireman, teacher
(fired for smoking in the can). At 20,
basketball scholarship to Ohio State,

but couldn't afford to take it.
His mother had just married Mac,
couldn't help him out. Ten years later,

she wanted to leave Mac (beat her),
had her bags packed, but no place to go —
my dad had just married my mother.

Faded photograph on my mother's dresser:
Dad leaning on a prop plane, leather helmet,
goggles — handsome, rakish,

must've been near 30 — but
he'd had rheumatic fever as a kid,
couldn't get a license.

*And with the severing of my head,
I lost all memory.*

*I forgot the dishes hurled against the wall,
the scissors, the sharps.*

*I forgot the summer I was seventeen
when my mother talked to the dead*

and wouldn't get out of bed.
I forgot I was the spitting image of my dad

who cried when I sang on stage with my high school class
because I looked so much like his mother.
I forgot. I forgot.

I had no head.
How could I remember?

I know during the Depression
he ironed his one pair of pants
every night with the palms

of his hands. I know in Ohio,
hillbillies like him were "snakes
in the grass," whether they

scabbed or not, whether they
twanged or not.

I know he didn't trust doctors.

I know she *functioned*.
But couldn't he see — ?

CLEAN FILL

Betty doesn't like to hear me say it, *Town
beyond saving.* She has a clipping now,
Gardening News Roundup — Compost Your Car.

It's true.
Bring me your tired refrigerators, your toasters,
your sorry plastic bags.

Shred them. Bacterialize them. Presto compo:
clean fill. EPA-approved. Junked cars
actually used to landscape Disney World.

Why not compost the mill? Betty says.

So how deep do you dig so run-off doesn't croak
the already scuzzy Tuscarawas?
Do the vacant stores get shredded, too,

and the decrepit high school whose bond levy
goes down every year anyway?

And what about the poor union schmoes

marching up Main Street, even five-year-olds
with signs, *Give My Dad's Job Back* — do we
throw them in, too? Blood is good for the soil.

How much bacteria does it take
to eat a dead steel mill?

PRAISE

At fourteen hitching from his uncle's farm into Wheeling
on a dead-end lead from one of the cousins, even
into his 60s, on his two-week vacations

with his maps and spiral pads
scouring every bone yard on both sides
of the Ohio.

And between vacations — nights
laying out white bread and ready-sliced
cheese, then too soon 5:00 a.m. and out the door

toting the lunchbox shaped like an iron lung,
like the Goodyear Aircraft hanger, nine hours
ropedancing the boss and the men, the din

and the backbiting. Then home to a wife
with "nerves," kids in our rooms,
radios full blast.

I'd left my father's bones behind and the widowed
steel town where I grew up — easily, I'd always said.

Let us praise Fulgencia Calzada.
He was the crowd. He was *there*.

And praise my father, always looking
for his own father. My lonely man.

St. Dymphna, *pray for us*,
poor sinners waiting at the Boys' Club
for handouts from United Way,

who put in 20 years
and didn't see it coming.
Forgive us

at the bank that wants its money back
for checks the mill reneged on.
Restore our retirement fund, our Workers' Comp.

In our last *illness*,

at the time of *death*,
have mercy.

Pray for us.

HIGHWAY TO NADA

The Erie Street Cemetery dips and rises —
less than a mile, as the crow flies,
from Dymphna's Shrine.

Calzada's stone: a four-foot granite cross
near the fence. Old coffee can,
a couple dried-up daisies.

Fulgencia Calzada,
Fallecio El Dia 11 de Julio 1937,
37 Edad.

Calzada, highway to *Nada*.
My dad was thirty-seven
that year, too.

Who brought the daisies?
Union records say Calzada's wife
is dead, no children.

I still want daisies
for my father. No, I want roses,
accolades of roses.

Paul Raphael Meltsner, *Industrial Landscape*, 1935

TWO

BACK HOME FROM NYC & OHIO, SITTING ON MY FRONT
STEPS, I'M LOOKING OUT AT THE VERGE, THAT GRASSY
STRIP BETWEEN THE SIDEWALK & THE STREET—IN OHIO
WE CALLED IT THE DEVIL'S HIGHWAY—& I'M THINKING
ABOUT AMERICA & ART & THE DEAD STEEL TOWN WHERE
I GREW UP & THE "MILL"—NOW A STORAGE YARD FOR
FRACKING PIPE, HUNDREDS OF MILES OF STEEL PIPE

1.

At the Guggenheim, Maurizio Cattalan's "America,"
an 18-karat gold toilet

a valuable, ostentatious object
that anyone can use—

fully functional... participatory...
unprecedented intimacy with a work of art

My friend Michael & I saw the line & we *declined*—though
we peeked in as a very Brooks Brothers guy emerged. The
gold throne gleamed ironically in its little understated stall.

2.

        & at the Massillon Museum (MassMu)
a homemade billy club, relic of the Little Steel strike,
leather, wood, lead, flexible handle, 1937, acquisition #94.127

           sticks & baseball bats vs. Republic's
rifles, bombs, machine guns

   & *a common role to play,*

        rescuing people trapped in blazing
buildings—by smashing windows or even doors

3.

& there is the grave of Fulgencio Calzada, long-forgotten striker shot in the back of the head, 1937, by Massillon city police hired on by "Little" Republic Steel. Massillon, Ohio, where I grew up, first time back in the fifteen years since my mother died, & at the Erie Street Cemetery, Calzada's tombstone is face down in the dirt, a four-foot granite cross, & I don't think it toppled in the wind.

4.

The verge—the city owns it, but I keep it tidy. Metaphor in there someplace. A devil to mow.

Always I'd go to Calzada's grave. My mother hovering at the window, *I'll have a heart attack if you're not back in an hour.* At the window in the dining room, by the table piled with coupons. But now she's resting in her own grave, & I was back to read a poem. *Don't talk about it, divided the town.* The great divide. The woman sawn in half.

5.

> Polar bears. Frogs. Steelworkers.
> Unions.
>
> On the verge of

6.

SOAR (Steelworkers Organization of Active Retirees) hosted
the event. To celebrate a book about the '37 strike—finally,
finally!—a brilliant author, & nice, too. I was the opening
gig. In MassMu's community room, two floors down from
acquisition #94.127. I read only my stanzas about the strike,
not about my family.

I couldn't tell what they thought of my poem, but I heard
gasps when I said Calzada's cross was down.

7.

>   Republic paid Calzada's wife $250
>   (liability) for the death of her husband.
>
>   The Steel Workers Organizing Committee
>   took up a collection for his cross (1937).

8.

>					billy club—leather, lead (what
>				contextualizes art?), handmade

9.

"America"—18-k version of a "readymade"

that anyone can use—as long as you
happen to be at the Gugg

democracy at its finest—

10.

endlessly long line, security guards

11.

Has "America"
changed your life?

12.

>   House on fire. Who or what
> knocked down the cross?

13.

& today in Stark County, Ohio, the retired steelworkers
(SOAR) have come to right Calzada's cross. I have a
friend who always says—not Michael, he'd never be that
presumptuous—*Bless you*. At the end of dinner, arms
outstretched, *Bless you*. As though he's some gold-plated guru.
But something rises up in me today. I want to bless them.

NOTES:

LITTLE STEEL

Few pages in the annals of labor surpass the 1937 "Little Steel" strike in viciousness, press distortion, suppression of basic civil rights, and police brutality. The findings of Congressional Committees, decisions of the NLRB, and judgments of the courts clearly testify to industry's reliance on lies, bribes, threats and brute force.... Under the ruthless leadership of Republic Steel's Tom Girdler, "Little Steel" announced its intention to "smash" any attempts at organization.... By late fall, most of the men were back at work without a contract.... The "Little Steel" strike had been broken, at least for the moment.

— *Then & Now*
United Steelworkers of America,
AFL-CIO-CLC

Stark County Coroner E.C. Reno ruled "excusable homicide" in the deaths of Nick Vathias and Fulgencia Calzada. Vathias's name is sometimes spelled Vadlas or Vadios in *The Evening*

Independent and elsewhere. Betty furnace information from Ruth Kane's *Wheat, Glass, Stone and Steel* (Massillon Bicentennial-Sesquicentennial Committee).

Account of St. Dymphna in the Rev. Sabine Baring-Gould's *The Lives of the Saints*, Vol. V (Edinburgh: John Grant, 1914). Additional information: publications from the National Shrine of St. Dymphna (first church in America dedicated to her honor, 5/15/1938), Massillon State Hospital, Massillon, Ohio.

(*Not many in...*) from William M. McCarty, "Think about it," *The Evening Independent*, 1986.

ACKNOWLEDGMENTS:

Little Steel first appeared in *Mudlark*, Issue No. 60 (2016). Thank you to Editor William Slaughter.

Back Home from NYC & Ohio, Sitting on My Front Steps, I'm Looking Out at the Verge, that Grassy Strip between the Sidewalk & the Street—in Ohio We Called it The Devil's Highway—*& I'm Thinking about America & Art & the Dead Steel Town where I Grew Up & the "Mill"—Now a Storage Yard for Fracking Pipe, Hundreds of Miles of Steel Pipe* first appeared in *The American Journal of Poetry*, Volume Four (2018). Thank you to Editor Robert Nazarene.

Philip Evergood, *American Tragedy*, 1937, oil, 29.5 x 39.5, private collection, photograph courtesy Terry Dintenfass Gallery.

Paul Raphael Meltsner, *Death of a Striker*, 1935, lithograph, 10.75 x 14.5 and *Industrial Landscape*, 1935, lithograph, 10.25 x 14.5, from the collection of Thomas Sodders, of the Labor Education & Arts Project Inc., Cleveland, Ohio.

Many thanks to editors Marc Estrin and Donna Bister for their political and literary vision in Fomite Press, for their down-home brilliance, for their unflagging belief in art's infectious power, and for believing in this book.

Kudos to designer W. David Powell. Kudos! Kudos!

Much gratitude for inspiration and cheering along the way: David Wojahn, Mark Halliday, Carol Westberg, Nora Mitchell, Robin Behn, Sharon Webster, my po-group PO, and so many others. And more than thanks to my husband Jan Schultz and my brother and sister-in-law John and Jan Burton for their love and encouragement.

Special thanks to Tom Sodders for his support of *Little Steel* and for his commitment to labor's ongoing struggle.

Thank you to SOAR 2711 (Steelworkers Organization of Active Retirees) for all their work.

Ahmed White—finally, finally—an exceptional study of the significance of the Little Steel strike. Thank you.

Thank you to actors/readers Anna Blackmer, Daniel Lusk, Angela Patten, Jim Reid, Andy Sacher, Al Salzman, and Sarah Sinnott, who joined me in a public reading of *Little Steel* at the old bristle factory, corner of Howard and Pine, Burlington, Vermont.

Thank you to the Vermont Arts Council, a State agency with funding from the National Endowment of the Arts, and to the Vermont Studio Center for their support during the completion of this work.

About the Author

Sue D. Burton has been awarded the Two Sylvias Press Poetry Prize (BOX, 2018), *Fourth Genre*'s Steinberg Prize, and a Vermont Arts Council grant. Her poetry has appeared in *Beloit Poetry Journal, Blackbird, Green Mountains Review, Mudlark, New Ohio Review,* and *Shenandoah*. She apprenticeship-trained as a physician assistant at the Vermont Women's Health Center and has an MFA in Writing from Vermont College.

Fomite

About Fomite

A fomite is a medium capable of transmitting infectious organisms from one individual to another.

"The activity of art is based on the capacity of people to be infected by the feelings of others." Tolstoy, *What Is Art?*

Writing a review on Amazon, Good Reads, Shelfari, Library Thing or other social media sites for readers will help the progress of independent publishing. To submit a review, go to the book page on any of the sites and follow the links for reviews. Books from independent presses rely on reader to reader communications.

For more information or to order any of our books, visit
http://www.fomitepress.com/FOMITE/Our_Books.html

More Titles from Fomite...

Novels
Joshua Amses — *During This, Our Nadir*
Joshua Amses — *Raven or Crow*
Joshua Amses — *The Moment Before an Injury*
Jaysinh Birjepatel — *The Good Muslim of Jackson Heights*
Jaysinh Birjepatel — *Nothing Beside Remains*
David Brizer — *Victor Rand*

Fomite

Paula Closson Buck — *Summer on the Cold War Planet*
Dan Chodorkoff — *Loisaida*
David Adams Cleveland — *Time's Betrayal*
Jaimee Wriston Colbert — *Vanishing Acts*
Roger Coleman — *Skywreck Afternoons*
Marc Estrin — *Hyde*
Marc Estrin — *Kafka's Roach*
Marc Estrin — *Speckled Vanities*
Zdravka Evtimova — *In the Town of Joy and Peace*
Zdravka Evtimova — *Sinfonia Bulgarica*
Daniel Forbes — *Derail This Train Wreck*
Greg Guma — *Dons of Time*
Richard Hawley — *The Three Lives of Jonathan Force*
Lamar Herrin — *Father Figure*
Michael Horner — *Damage Control*
Ron Jacobs — *All the Sinners Saints*
Ron Jacobs — *Short Order Frame Up*
Ron Jacobs — *The Co-conspirator's Tale*
Scott Archer Jones — *A Rising Tide of People Swept Away*
Julie Justicz — *A Boy Called Home*
Maggie Kast — *A Free Unsullied Land*
Darrell Kastin — *Shadowboxing with Bukowski*
Coleen Kearon — *Feminist on Fire*
Coleen Kearon — *#triggerwarning*
Jan Englis Leary — *Thicker Than Blood*
Diane Lefer — *Confessions of a Carnivore*

Fomite

Rob Lenihan — *Born Speaking Lies*
Colin Mitchell — *Roadman*
Ilan Mochari — *Zinsky the Obscure*
Peter Nash — *Parsimony*
Peter Nash — *The Perfection of Things*
Gregory Papadoyiannis — *The Baby Jazz*
Andy Potok — *My Father's Keeper*
Kathryn Roberts — *Companion Plants*
Robert Rosenberg — *Isles of the Blind*
Fred Russell — *Rafi's World*
Ron Savage — *Voyeur in Tangier*
David Schein — *The Adoption*
Lynn Sloan — *Principles of Navigation*
L.E. Smith — *The Consequence of Gesture*
L.E. Smith — *Travers' Inferno*
L.E. Smith — *Untimely RIPped*
Bob Sommer — *A Great Fullness*
Tom Walker — *A Day in the Life*
Susan V. Weiss — *My God, What Have We Done?*
Peter M. Wheelwright — *As It Is On Earth*
Suzie Wizowaty — *The Return of Jason Green*

Poetry

Anna Blackmer — *Hexagrams*
Antonello Borra — *Alfabestiario*

Fomite

Antonello Borra — *AlphaBetaBestiaro*
Sue Burton — *Little Steel*
David Cavanagh — *Cycling in Plato's Cave*
James Connolly — *Picking Up the Bodies*
Greg Delanty — *Loosestrife*
Mason Drukman — *Drawing on Life*
J. C. Ellefson — *Foreign Tales of Exemplum and Woe*
Tina Escaja — *Caida Libre/Free Fall*
Anna Faktorovich — *Improvisational Arguments*
Barry Goldensohn — *Snake in the Spine, Wolf in the Heart*
Barry Goldensohn — *The Hundred Yard Dash Man*
Barry Goldensohn — *The Listener Aspires to the Condition of Music*
R. L. Green — *When — You Remember Deir Yassin*
Kate Magill — *Roadworthy Creature, Roadworthy Craft*
Tony Magistrale — *Entanglements*
Andreas Nolte — *Mascha: The Poems of Mascha Kaléko*
Sherry Olson — *Four-Way Stop*
David Polk — *Drinking the River*
Phliip Ramp — *The Melancholy Of A Life As The Joy Of Living It Slowly Chills*
Janice Miller Potter — *Meanwell*
Joseph D. Reich — *Connecting the Dots to Shangrila*
Joseph D. Reich — *The Hole That Runs Through Utopia*
Joseph D. Reich — *The Housing Market*
Joseph D. Reich — *The Derivation of Cowboys and Indians*
Kennet Rosen and Richard Wilson — *Gomorrah*

Fomite

Fred Rosenblum — *Vietnumb*
David Schein — *My Murder and Other Local News*
Harold Schweizer — *Miriam's Book*
Scott T. Starbuck — *Industrial Oz*
Scott T. Starbuck — *Hawk on Wire*
Seth Steinzor — *Among the Lost*
Seth Steinzor — *To Join the Lost*
Susan Thomas — *The Empty Notebook Interrogates Itself*
Susan Thomas — *In the Sadness Museum*
Paolo Valesio and Todd Portnowitz — *Midnight in Spoleto*
Sharon Webster — *Everyone Lives Here*
Tony Whedon — *The Tres Riches Heures*
Tony Whedon — *The Falkland Quartet*
Claire Zoghb — *Dispatches from Everest*

Stories

Jay Boyer — *Flight*
Michael Cocchiarale — *Still Time*
Michael Cocchiarale — *Here Is Ware*
Neil Connelly — *In the Wake of Our Vows*
Catherine Zobal Dent — *Unfinished Stories of Girls*
Zdravka Evtimova —*Carts and Other Stories*
John Michael Flynn — *Off to the Next Wherever*
Derek Furr — *Semitones*
Derek Furr — *Suite for Three Voices*
Elizabeth Genovise — *Where There Are Two or More*

Fomite

Andrei Guriuanu — *Body of Work*
Zeke Jarvis — *In A Family Way*
Jan Englis Leary — *Skating on the Vertical*
Marjorie Maddox — *What She Was Saying*
William Marquess — *Boom-shacka-lacka*
Gary Miller — *Museum of the Americas*
Jennifer Anne Moses — *Visiting Hours*
Martin Ott — *Interrogations*
Jack Pulaski — *Love's Labours*
Charles Rafferty — *Saturday Night at Magellan's*
Ron Savage — *What We Do For Love*
Fred Skolnik — *Americans and Other Stories*
Lynn Sloan — *This Far Isn't Far Enough*
L.E. Smith — *Views Cost Extra*
Caitlin Hamilton Summie — *To Lay To Rest Our Ghosts*
Susan Thomas — *Among Angelic Orders*
Tom Walker — *Signed Confessions*
Silas Dent Zobal — *The Inconvenience of the Wings*

Odd Birds

Micheal Breiner — *the way none of this happened*
J. C. Ellefson — *Under the Influence*
David Ross Gunn — *Cautionary Chronicles*
Andrei Guriuanu — *The Darkest City*
Gail Holst-Warhaft — *The Fall of Athens*
Roger Leboitz — *A Guide to the Western Slopes and the Outlying Area*

Fomite

dug Nap — *Artsy Fartsy*
Delia Bell Robinson — *A Shirtwaist Story*
Peter Schumann — *Bread & Sentences*
Peter Schumann — *Charlotte Salomon*
Peter Schumann — *Faust 3*
Peter Schumann — *Planet Kasper, Volumes One and Two*
Peter Schumann — *We*

Plays
Stephen Goldberg — *Screwed and Other Plays*
Michele Markarian — *Unborn Children of America*

Essays
Robert Sommer — *Losing Francis: Essays on the Wars at Home*

Made in the USA
Middletown, DE
27 November 2019